SHEPHERD SPY

by simon drew

ANTIQUE COLLECTORS' CLUB

ISBN 978-1-905377-16-9

British Library Cataloguing-in-Publication Data
A catalogue record for this book is available from the British Library

Printed in China
for the Antique Collectors' Club Ltd., Woodbridge, Suffolk

INTRODUCTION

This is the story of how a detective-cum-spy of very special prowess tracks down his enemy. Extraordinary ingenuity and stealth assist him in his task of rooting out evil, pursuing it doggedly and resolving to rid the world of its blight. He is persistent. He is cunning. He is undaunted. He appears sheepish. Actually his diary reveals that he's rubbish.

Here is a picture of our hero:

At the end of the book there are details of the puzzles hidden in the story.

DAY ONE: the diary
BEGINNING THE GAME

A new year starts: my work begins.
They call me Shepherd Spy.
I fight with many enemies:
I hear you asking why . . . . .

The world is full of vicious sheep,
I'm sure its no surprise.
They'd pull the wool right off your
                              back
and over both your eyes.

Their aim is total dominance:
they want us all enslaved.
We'll never sleep secure again
until the world is saved.

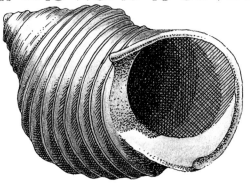

hair of the dog:
(after the
new year
celebrations

DAY TWO: RESOLVE

And so I'll travel anywhere
to stop the Devil's deeds.
    (Buy more breakfast cereals/
    basil / parsley seeds/
    beer and salt / bananas/plums/
    lentils/ beans and maize).
Clear the rash of criminals
so some may safely graze.

sheep safely glazing

DAY THREE:
INTO WAR

The escalator's going down/
(airport called Heathrow)/
my coffee in a plastic cup/
sandwiches (to go).

I've had a call from tundraland/
an ancient Romanov
(but did I water all the plants?
Is the gas turned off?)

Something strange is going on:
he couldn't tell me what.
Investigators, need my help,
(he says they've lost the plot).

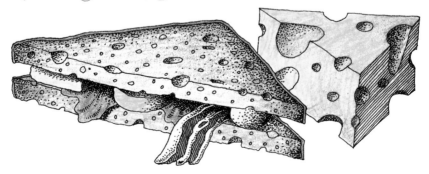

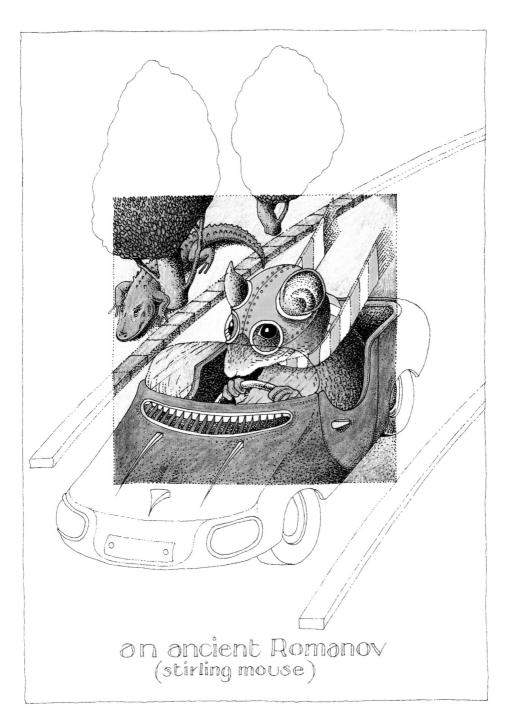

an ancient Romanov
(stirling mouse)

DAY FOUR :
GOSH

Arrive/suspicious happenings/
legs are flashing by,
somewhere high up/blurred sheep
rush/
too fast to catch the eye.

And as the whirlwind dies away
they haven't left a trace.
But then I realise what it was:
I've seen a tall sheep race.

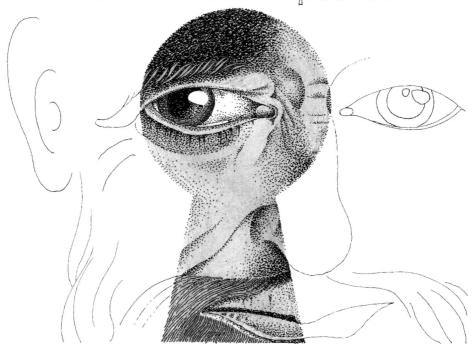

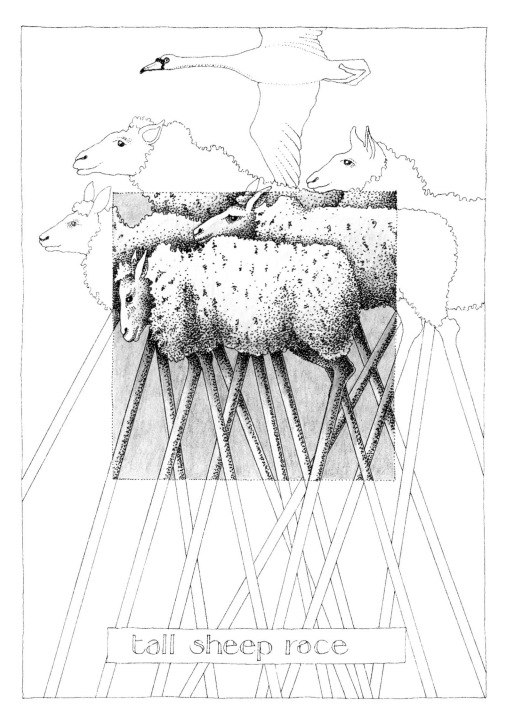

tall sheep race

DAY FIVE:
HUNT

I've found an ovine family
searching for a son/
"the blackest sheep we've ever had/
the only missing one."

(So could their son be prodigal?
And could they all be right?)
Snooping/hunting/nothing found
but woolly sheep in white.

So where do black sheep go at
night?
Or do they disappear?
Does this miscreant exist?
Have we a black hole here?

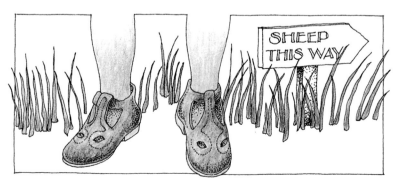

DAY SIX:
TAKING A BREATHER

(I must repair my luggage strap/
it's nearly broken through/
I also need a baseball cap/
I think I might buy two).

Taking stock of all I've learnt,
what's the problem here?
First I need a reindeer steak/
perhaps some polar beer.

polar beer

our hero wearing
two baseball caps:
one is facing
forwards (unfashionable)
and one is facing
backwards (unfashionable).

DAY SEVEN:
OUTSTANDING EVIDENCE

Searching through the evidence:
a copy of the Times/
a pair of scissors/cuttings too/
pennies, pounds and dimes.

Adding up the coins I've found
they total fourteen pounds.
The name of Russell comes to mind
(for that's how paper sounds).

I've made a stew of all these clues/
reduced them to the bone.
The answer stares me in the face:
scissors, paper, stone.

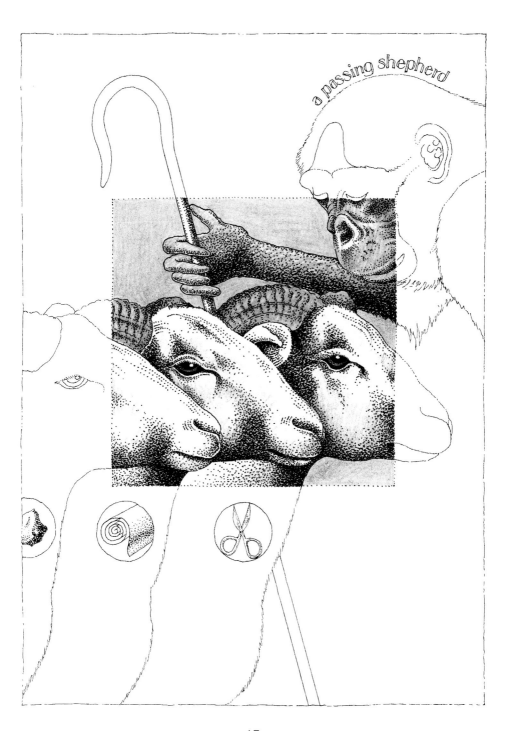

a passing shepherd

DAY EIGHT:
NO GOING BACK

I've needed just a little help/
an old friend lives nearby/
he's been a naval admiral
(I've never wondered why).

(Soon I need a chemist's shop –
a blister on my heel/
and something for big-headedness/
I can't help how I feel).

"Rid this world of sheep of shame,
a menace to us all",
is all my friend will ever say,
(his brain is rather small).

And so encouraged/progress made/
with evil in my sights,
I catch the Sherwood Forest train
to see some men in tights.

my friend:

a wolf in ship's clothing

DAY NINE:
ROBIN THE CRITIC

I find a motley gathering
and ask if they agree:
"the world is full of evil sheep?"
They simply stare at me.

(If I may use a metaphor)
they show me to the door.
They say they steal from wealthy
men
and give it to the poor!

Far from me to criticize,
but what's the point of that
when evil sheep are roaming free?
(and what a stupid hat).

DAY TEN:
AMMO

So now I'm off to Belgian shores
(forgot to mend that strap)
(remember: compass/walking stick/
a torch and local map).

I've two fat cousins near Ostend
whose chocolate shop is famed.
They've rid the hills of sweet-toothed
                              lambs,
(though Belgian grass was blamed).

My cousins' method, told to me,
involves a poisoned spray.
They squirt the sweets that sheep most
                              like:
I take a box away.

choc absorbers

OX CHOX

DAY ELEVEN :
INTERVAL

The weapons, safely in a bag,
could rid a town of sheep.
I tiptoe through the darkened lanes/
the terrorists asleep.

Then, as a lamb awakes to stretch,
I creep out from my hole
and slip a special sweet of doom
into its cornflake bowl.

It gobbles up the dainty dish
as though it had no care :
then rolls around upon its back,
its legs up in the air.

But in an hour the lamb gets up
unsteady on its feet.
The poison used has been too weak.
I beat a fast retreat.

cereal killer

sheepwreck

DAY TWELVE: LITTLE BEASTIE

Helter skelter/ lost in thought/
I run/ don't know how long.
But this I know – the clever plot
has gone a little wrong.

I'll try to take a better route
(for what you think it's worth)
but fall into a dirty heap:
I've struck a mound of earth.

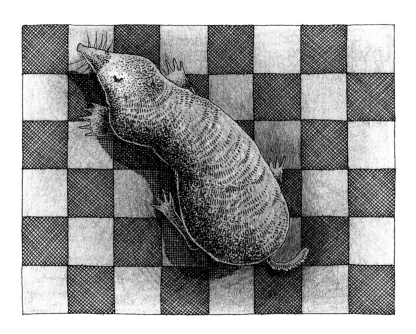

26

DAY THIRTEEN: WRITING

On getting up, I realise
a shadow has appeared/
my oldest friend from Germany
disguised in hat and beard.

"I'm looking for the Evil One,"
(for that is now my aim).
And he says: "What coincidence;
my thoughts were just the same."

"But please go on ahead of me,"
he says with some regret.
"I'm writing choral symphonies
and haven't finished yet."

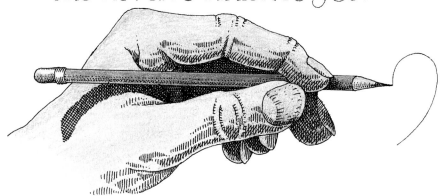

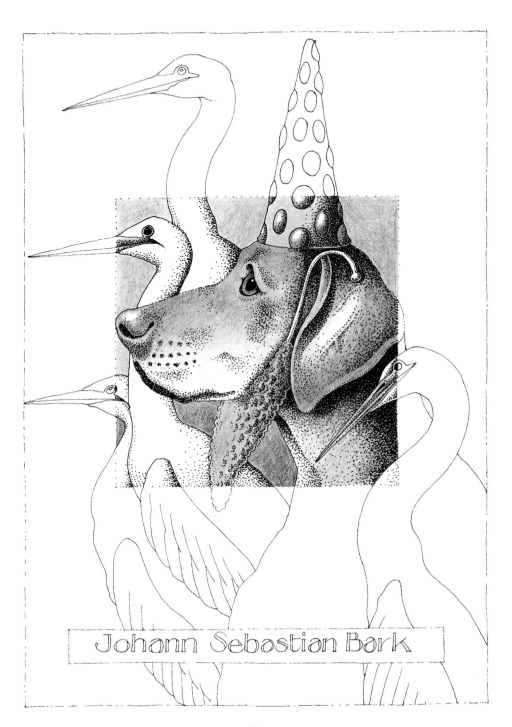

Johann Sebastian Bark

DAY FOURTEEN:
AND SO TO PASTA

So back to finding enemies/
I know where I will look:
They like Italian restaurants:
you see — they cannot cook.

cleopatra's
noodle

DAY FIFTEEN:
YODELLING

Inside a foul trattoria
that smells of rotten scabs
I find a sheep and draw my sword
to make myself kebabs.

But... lying on my back again /
a coup de grace he dealt.
I've come across the only sheep
that has a judo belt.

At last, I've found the Evil One ;
I've heard about his skills.
I must not let him get away /
prepare for daring thrills.

warsheep

DAY SIXTEEN:
SEEING IS BELIEVING

Yet in a trice he leaves the room/
I catch a vital glimpse:
for with that artificial leg
I'll know him by his limps.

this is his friend

DAY SEVENTEEN: TRACK YOU

Through the streets and alleyways
we dodge and hop and skid.
People stare with open mouths
and say: "I never did".

I nearly grab him by his tail
but what makes matters worse
is how the swine's evaded me
by clinging to a hearse.

DAY EIGHTEEN:
ATTEMPTS TO BE REGAL

(My blister's very painful now/
 I need that bandage soon/
 I notice in the diary:
 bank holiday/full moon).

The Evil One has reappeared:
he thinks I haven't seen.
He's found a giant king and queen
to hide himself between.

FROG'S PAWN

DAY NINETEEN:
TACIT

So now I have him in my sights:
I'll cut off his escape.
I'll creep up from behind him and
I'll crush him (like a grape).

I hack my way through countless pawns:
A bishop leaps aside.
The evil one has noticed me:
the Spy has been espied.

"Should I move my castle here?"
he's started a debate!
His tactics are surprising me
and soon I lose (check mate).

a spectator

it was very difficult to see past his castle

DAY TWENTY:
I SHOW BELIEF

And so without consulting him
I put the pieces back:
the board is set for my revenge.
I tell him I am 'black.'

Although he's made some simple moves,
he's played the game before.
But I will not be fooled again
I'll even up the score.

a score

42

DAY TWENTY ONE: OVERTAKE

Without a thought I move my knight
and take a pawn with ease.
He wheels his bishop back a square;
this move was meant to tease.

The game is turning serious
and as I touch my king
a light appears above my head
and birds begin to sing.

A guiding form is aiding me:
this angel helps my game
and though I've seen its face before
I've never known its name.

my furry dogmother

DAY TWENTY TWO: NOTHING'S FINAL

My score of games is forty nine
and his is forty five;
I think we'll never end the match
as long as we're alive.

I'm finding pleasure playing him
and so I must confess
I'm happy that the fates decreed
we'd play eternal chess.

THE END ?

EPILOGUE
The Great Mystery

A secret hiding place is buried in the story. If you can discover where this place is please write and tell me. The first few will receive one of the original pages from this book, mounted and signed. You are seeking a very specific location somewhere in England.

The address to write to is:
The Simon Drew Gallery, 13 foss street, dartmouth, devon, TQ6 9DR, England.

Additional puzzles:
Somewhere in each main drawing an extra animal (not sheep or dog) appears which is hidden in the text on the opposite page. For instance in the line "He was putting on a hat", a 'wasp' may be taken from the text and illustrated in the drawing. For your own amusement you may like to find them all: if you would like a list of these hidden animals please write to the address above. I hope you have enjoyed the book. S.D.

48